HOW THE EXECUTIVE BRANCH WORKS

by Rebecca E. Hirsch

Content Consultant
Dr. Arnold Shober
Associate Professor of Government
Lawrence University

Core Library

An Imprint of Abdo Publishing
www.abdopublishing.com

www.abdopublishing.com

Published by Abdo Publishing, a division of ABDO, PO Box 398166, Minneapolis, Minnesota 55439. Copyright © 2015 by Abdo Consulting Group, Inc. International copyrights reserved in all countries. No part of this book may be reproduced in any form without written permission from the publisher. Core Library™ is a trademark and logo of Abdo Publishing.

Printed in the United States of America, North Mankato, Minnesota
092014
012015

THIS BOOK CONTAINS
RECYCLED MATERIALS

Cover Photo: Thinkstock
Interior Photos: Thinkstock, 1, 34, 40; MSgt Cecilio Ricardo, 4; Doug Mills/AP Images, 6; John Trumbull/US Capitol, 8, 14; Shutterstock Images, 10; Emanuel Leutze, 13; Robert Churchill/Thinkstock, 18; David Phillip/AP Images, 23; Bettmann/Corbis, 24; J. Scott Applewhite/AP Images, 26, 38; Brooks Kraft/Corbis, 29; Barry Thumma/AP Images, 31; Pete Souza, 45

Editor: Heather C. Hudak
Series Designer: Becky Daum

Library of Congress Control Number: 2014944231

Cataloging-in-Publication Data
Hirsch, Rebecca E.
  How the executive branch works / Rebecca E. Hirsch.
    p. cm. -- (How the US government works)
  ISBN 978-1-62403-635-4 (lib. bdg.)
  Includes bibliographical references and index.
  1. United States--Politics and government--Juvenile literature. 2. Presidents--United States--Juvenile literature. 3. Executive departments--United States--Juvenile literature. I. Title.
  351--dc23
                                                        2014944231

CONTENTS

CHAPTER ONE

The Presidency

O n January 20, 2009, Barack Obama walked
onto a balcony outside the US Capitol. It
was inauguration day, and an enormous
crowd had gathered. Everyone hushed as Obama
took the oath of office. He promised to perform his
job to the best of his abilities. The crowd burst into
cheers and applause.

Barack Obama's first inauguration was on January 20, 2009. He
was sworn in as the forty-fourth president of the United States.

George W. Bush's second inauguration was on January 20, 2005.

Every four years, the United States inaugurates a president. The president is not born into the office, like a king or queen. The president does not seize the office by force, like a military dictator. Instead the president is elected by the people.

Creating the Government

A group known as the Founding Fathers set out to create a government for the new United States in May of 1787. The United States had just fought and won the American Revolutionary War (1775–1783) against

Great Britain. Many Americans did not want to be ruled by a king. The writers of the US Constitution wanted to be sure no single person or group could ever take control of the US government.

The Founding Fathers decided to form a republic. In this type of government, the people decide who will rule them. They do this by electing leaders to represent them.

The founders wrote the rules for setting up the new government in a document called the Constitution. The Constitution is the highest law of the United States.

The Founding Fathers

From May to September 1787, a group of political leaders met in Philadelphia to write a new constitution. The meeting was called the Constitutional Convention. The Founding Fathers' goal was to protect life, liberty, and property. They also set out to create a government for the new nation. The men in attendance included George Washington, James Madison, and Alexander Hamilton. The youngest, at age 26, was Jonathan Dayton. The oldest, at age 81, was Benjamin Franklin. The men came from all 13 states, except Rhode Island.

The Founding Fathers drafted the Declaration of Independence in 1776. This document said the 13 US colonies viewed themselves as free from British rule.

It divides the government into three branches: the executive branch, the legislative branch, and the judicial branch. Each branch has certain powers.

The Three Branches of Government

The president is head of the executive branch. The executive branch also includes the vice president and all the people who work for the president and vice president. Their job is to enforce the laws.

The legislative branch is made up of the Senate and the House of Representatives. Together they are called Congress. Congress has the power to make new laws.

The judicial branch is made up of the courts. This branch includes the US Supreme Court, the highest court in the country. It makes sure all laws uphold the Constitution.

Changing the Constitution

The US Constitution was designed to be changed. A change to the Constitution is called an amendment. Two-thirds of Congress must propose an amendment to the Constitution. Then three-fourths of the state legislatures must ratify the proposal. The first ten amendments are called the Bill of Rights. They were ratified on December 15, 1971. The Bill of Rights is a list of freedoms for all people. They include free speech and the freedom to practice one's own religion. Other amendments to the Constitution abolished slavery and gave the right to vote to African Americans, women, and people as young as 18 years of age.

We the People

insure domestic Tranquility provide for the common
and our Posterity, do ordain and establish this Con

Article I

Section 1. All legislative Powers herein granted shall be vested in a Congress of the United States, which shall con
of Representatives.

Section 2. The House of Representatives shall be composed of Members chosen every second Year by the People of the
in each State shall have Qualifications requisite for Electors of the most numerous Branch of the State Legislature.

No Person shall be a Representative who shall not have attained to the Age of twenty five Years, and been an In
who shall not, when elected, be an Inhabitant of that State in which he shall be chosen.

Representatives and direct Taxes shall be apportioned among the several States which may be included within this
Numbers, which shall be determined by adding to the whole Number of free Persons, including those bound to Service
not taxed, three fifths of all other Persons. The actual Enumeration shall be made within three Years after the first
and within every subsequent Term of ten Years, in such Manner as they shall by Law direct. The Number of R
thirty Thousand, but each State shall have at Least one Representative; and until such enumeration shall be made, th
entitled to chuse three, Massachusetts eight, Rhode Island and Providence Plantations one, Connecticut five, New
Delaware one, Maryland six, Virginia ten, North Carolina five, South Carolina five, and Georgia three

When vacancies happen in the Representation from any State, the Executive Authority thereof shall
of Representatives shall chuse their Speaker and other Officers, and shall have the sole Power of Im

The History of the Executive Branch

Part of the US Constitution creates the job of president. The Constitution states that the president commands the military and enforces the laws. But beyond that, the Constitution has very little to say about the president's job.

The writers of the Constitution argued about how much power a president should have. In the end, they decided not to provide a lot of detail. Most of

The US Constitution was ratified in 1788.

the men assumed George Washington would be the first president. Washington was a well-known and respected military leader during the revolution. The Founding Fathers trusted Washington would figure out how to do a good job.

Washington's Presidency

Washington knew he was creating a model for other presidents to follow. He wanted to be grand without seeming like a king. Washington bowed to guests and rode in a white carriage. But he did not use a fancy title, such as "His Highness." He chose to be called "Mr. President."

Washington also had to decide how to run the executive branch. He chose people to advise him and help him do his job. He made Alexander Hamilton the secretary of the treasury. Hamilton would be responsible for the country's money and financial matters. Washington chose Thomas Jefferson to be his secretary of state. Jefferson would be responsible for US foreign affairs, or issues of US interest in other

George Washington was commander-in-chief of the Continental Army in the American Revolutionary War.

nations. There were only four officially appointed advisors to the president. Even though Washington had helpers, he made the decisions.

Washington served two four-year terms as president between 1789 and 1797. At the end of his second term, he stepped down. He set a tradition of presidents only serving two terms.

The Changing Presidency

In the early years of the country, the executive branch was small. There were only a few departments. Each department handled a different aspect of the US

Washington resigned as commander-in-chief of the Continental Army on December 23, 1783.

government, such as dealing with other countries, money matters, and conflicts.

In those early years, presidents were not very powerful. Washington felt his main task was to appoint people to government jobs. He felt it inappropriate to comment on legislation until it came to his desk for a signature.

A few early presidents took more control. Thomas Jefferson was president from 1801 to 1809. He oversaw the Louisiana Purchase in 1803. Andrew Jackson, who was president from 1829 to

1837, vetoed 12 bills. This is more than all the previous presidents combined. A veto is when a president refuses to pass a bill already passed by Congress.

Abraham Lincoln was another powerful president. He was president from 1861 to 1865. Lincoln expanded the military during the American Civil War (1861–1865). At the beginning of the Civil War, the US Army had about 16,000 soldiers. By the end of the war,

The Louisiana Purchase

President Thomas Jefferson wanted to acquire the Louisiana Territory from France. The territory included 828,000 square miles (2.1 million square km) of land west of the Mississippi River. But no part of the US Constitution said a president could buy new land. Jefferson believed in strictly following the Constitution. Changing the Constitution to allow the president to make the purchase would take a long time. After much thought, he went ahead with the deal. In 1803 Jefferson bought the land for $15 million. With that deal, Jefferson expanded the size of the country. He also paved the way for future presidents to increase the power of the executive branch.

Abraham Lincoln

During the American Civil War, Abraham Lincoln blocked southern ports, spent money on weapons and ships, expanded the army, and held prisoners without charges or a trial. None of these powers were granted in the US Constitution. Lincoln felt he was upholding his oath to "preserve, protect, and defend the Constitution of the United States." Like all presidents, Lincoln vowed this oath during his inauguration.

the army had more than 1 million soldiers.

In the 1900s, presidents started to expand the size of the executive branch. President Theodore Roosevelt and later presidents, such as Woodrow Wilson and Herbert Hoover, saw their office as an active part of the legislative process. Over time, Americans came to think of their presidents as being responsible for day-to-day well-being, national security, and money matters.

Franklin Delano Roosevelt served as president from 1933 to 1945. He made the presidency an even more active role in the 1930s. At the time, many people were out of work. Many banks, stores, and factories had closed. This time in history is known as the Great Depression. Roosevelt put together a package of programs to help people. The package was called the New Deal. It introduced a national minimum wage. It also included Social Security. This is a program that pays money to people who are retired, jobless, or unable to work.

EXPLORE ONLINE

Chapter Two touches on George Washington and the power of the president. The website below focuses on Washington. As you know, every source is different. How is the information on the website different from the information in this chapter? What information is the same? How do the two sources present information differently? What can you learn from this website?

President George Washington
www.mycorelibrary.com/executive-branch

CHAPTER THREE

Becoming President

Who can become president? Each president must have been born a US citizen. They must be at least 35 years old. And they must have lived in the United States for at least 14 years.

Presidents are elected to four-year terms. No person can be elected more than two times.

Any person meeting the eligibility requirements can become president of the United States.

Franklin Delano Roosevelt

George Washington stepped down after two terms as president. Other presidents followed his lead, even though there was no law keeping them from serving more terms. Franklin Delano Roosevelt was the only president elected to more than two terms. He came into office in 1933 during the Great Depression. He was elected four times. Roosevelt died in 1945 during his fourth term. In 1951 the Twenty-second Amendment to the US Constitution was ratified. It states that no president can be elected to more than two terms.

Electing the President

The Founding Fathers disagreed about how the president should be chosen. Some thought the citizens should vote. Some believed Congress should choose. Others thought the decision should be up to the states. In the end, the Founding Fathers compromised. They created the Electoral College.

Members of the Electoral College are called electors. Electors pledge their support to a party's candidate

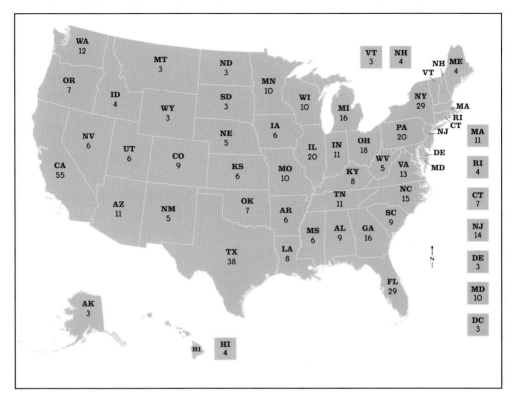

Electors for President

This map shows the number of electoral votes for each state in the 2012 presidential election. Based on this map, why might presidential candidates campaign to win electoral votes in some states and not others?

for president. People vote for the elector who supports the person they want to become president. The electors then place their vote for president. A candidate must receive 270 of the 538 electoral votes to become president. Electors also elect a vice president along with the president.

The 2000 Election

In the 2000 presidential election, Al Gore won the popular vote. But the popular vote in the state of Florida was close. The votes had to be recounted. The winner in Florida would win all of Florida's electoral votes. That person would win the election. Recounts stopped and started many times as officials tried to decide how to proceed. Finally the Florida Supreme Court got involved. It ruled to extend the timeline for the recount. But the US Supreme Court overruled the decision. A week later, the Florida Supreme Court ordered a recount. And the US Supreme Court put a hold on it. Eventually the US Supreme Court chose not to do a recount. It gave Florida's electoral votes to George W. Bush.

Each state has as many electors as they have representatives and senators in Congress. This number is based on the population of each state. States with larger populations have more electors. The process for selecting electors varies by state.

Sometimes one presidential candidate wins the popular vote but loses the election. The other candidate wins the most electoral votes, the votes cast by the electors. This happens because all of a state's electoral votes

George W. Bush and Al Gore took part in three presidential debates in October 2000.

go to the same candidate. The winner is the person with the most electoral votes. Four presidents were elected after losing the popular vote: John Quincy Adams, Rutherford B. Hayes, Benjamin Harrison, and George W. Bush.

Presidential Succession

If a president dies in office or steps down, the vice president becomes president. This has happened nine times in the country's history. Eight presidents have died in office and been replaced by the vice

Gerald Ford, right, served as vice president under Richard Nixon, left.

president. Gerald Ford became president when Richard Nixon stepped down.

If the vice president cannot take over, the next person in line is the Speaker of the House of Representatives, a presiding officer elected by the House. After that is the President pro tempore of the Senate, who performs a similar role in the Senate. Next are the Secretary of State, the Secretary of the Treasury, and the Secretary of Defense.

The US Constitution outlines the qualifications to be president. It says:

> *No person except a natural born citizen, or a citizen of the United States, at the time of the adoption of this Constitution, shall be eligible to the office of President; neither shall any person be eligible to that office who shall not have attained to the age of thirty five years, and been fourteen years a resident within the United States.*

Source: "Constitution of the United States." United States Senate. United States Senate, n.d. Web. Accessed June 19, 2014.

Changing Minds

Take a position on whether people under the age of 35 should be able to become president. Imagine your best friend has the opposite opinion. Write an essay trying to change your friend's mind. Make sure you explain your opinion and your reasons for it. Include facts and details to support your reasons.

CHAPTER FOUR

The Executive Branch at Work

More than 2.7 million people work for the federal government. Most of these people work for the executive branch.

The President's Job

The presidency is several jobs in one. The president commands the armed forces. As commander in chief, the president decides whether or not to send troops into combat. The president also is the US head of

The president of the United States is the leader of the country with the world's largest economy and a very powerful military.

The President's Salary and Benefits

The president earns $400,000 a year. He travels by air on one of two special jets known as Air Force One and by car in an armored limousine. The president works and lives in the 132-room White House. His office is called the Oval Office. It is located in the West Wing of the White House. The president and his family live on the second floor of the White House. The White House has a bowling alley, tennis court, swimming pool, and movie theater.

state. He meets with the leaders of other countries and negotiates treaties, or formal agreements between two or more countries.

The president runs the executive branch. It is his job to enforce thousands of laws. The president appoints many people to top jobs in the executive branch. He appoints federal judges, ambassadors, top military leaders, and heads of government departments.

The president can also issue executive orders. Executive orders are a lot like laws, but they do not have to be approved by Congress. With an executive order, the president can make sure laws are

Sonia Sotomayor was sworn in as a Supreme Court judge on August 8, 2009, after being nominated for the job by President Obama.

carried out. But executive orders can only affect the activities of the executive branch. The Emancipation Proclamation was an executive order. It was issued by President Abraham Lincoln during the American Civil War. It freed all slaves in parts of the United States that were still in rebellion.

The Vice President's Job

The main job of the vice president is to step in if the president dies, becomes very ill, or resigns. This has

Ending School Segregation

In 1954 the US Supreme Court ruled to end school segregation. This is the separation of people by race, class, or group. Ending segregation meant black students and white students would attend school together. In 1957 the governor of Arkansas defied the vote. He ordered the Arkansas National Guard to keep nine black students from entering an all-white high school.

To enforce the law, President Dwight D. Eisenhower issued an executive order. He sent federal troops to the school. Escorted by the troops, the nine students safely entered the school.

happened ten times. Eight presidents have died in office, and one has stepped down. In 1985 George H. W. Bush was acting president for eight hours while Ronald Reagan had surgery.

The vice president also serves as president of the Senate. If half the senators oppose a bill and the other half support it, the vice president casts the deciding vote.

In recent years, vice presidents have been given more to do. As vice president under Bill Clinton, Al Gore advised

President Ronald Reagan, right, chose George H. W. Bush, left, to run for vice president.

the president on foreign policy and environmental issues. As vice president under George W. Bush, Dick Cheney advised the president on foreign affairs.

The Cabinet and Executive Office of the President

The president has several teams of advisors. One team is called the Cabinet. It is made up of the heads of the departments of the executive branch. Most Cabinet members take the title of secretary. The head of the Justice Department is known as the

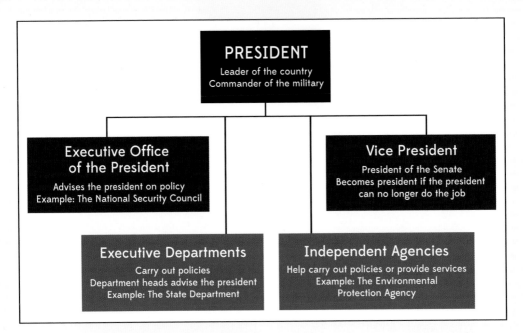

The Executive Branch

Study this diagram. How does the information presented compare to what you have learned from the text about the structure of the executive branch? How are the descriptions similar to what you have learned? How are they different?

attorney general. This role is filled by a high-ranking law-enforcement official. Cabinet members are appointed by the president and approved by the Senate.

The Cabinet has many departments. They include agriculture, energy, and transportation.

The president has another team of advisors known as the Executive Office of the President. This team includes the National Security Council, a group of top military and foreign policy leaders. They advise the president on issues of national security.

FURTHER EVIDENCE

Chapter Four has quite a bit of information about the job of the executive branch. What is one of the main jobs of the executive branch? What key evidence supports this point? Go to the section on the president of the United States at the website below. Find a quote from the website that supports the chapter's main point. Does the quote support an existing piece of evidence in the chapter? Or does it add a new one?

The White House: The Executive Branch
www.mycorelibrary.com/executive-branch

CHAPTER FIVE

Working Together

The executive branch works with the other two branches of government. Power is shared among the branches. This is known as a separation of power. To prevent one branch from having too much power, each branch can partially check, or hold back, the power of the other branches. This is done through a system of checks and balances.

The United States Capitol is home to the legislative branch, also known as Congress.

Checks and Balances

The US Constitution gives Congress the power to pass laws. But the president can check Congress's power. After a bill is approved by Congress, the president must sign it. If the president does not like a bill, he or she can veto it.

Congress can also check the president's power. Congress can override a veto if two-thirds of both houses agree. And Congress can refuse to pass a bill. Additionally, although the president can initiate a treaty, he or she needs Congress's approval to

Who Declares War?

According to the US Constitution, the president commands the armed forces. But only Congress can declare war. Still, presidents can send US troops to fight without asking Congress. But the president has 48 hours to tell Congress of any plans to send troops into action.

Congress declared war in 1941 after Japanese planes attacked Pearl Harbor, a military base in Hawaii. In response President Franklin Roosevelt asked Congress for a declaration of war. Congress declared war, and the United States officially entered World War II (1939–1945).

The Three Branches of Federal Government

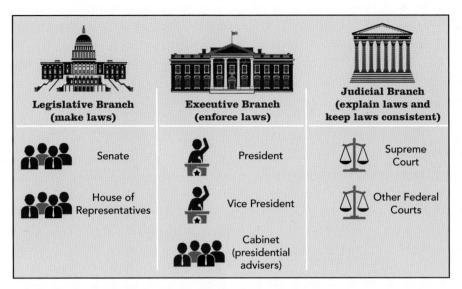

Legislative Branch (make laws)
Senate
House of Representatives

Executive Branch (enforce laws)
President
Vice President
Cabinet (presidential advisers)

Judicial Branch (explain laws and keep laws consistent)
Supreme Court
Other Federal Courts

Study this diagram. How does the information presented compare to what you have learned from the text about separation of powers? How do the legislative and judicial branches check the power of the president? How does the president check the power of the other two branches?

complete it. And the Senate can approve or reject people the president has appointed to top jobs in the executive branch.

The system of checks and balances also applies to the judicial branch and the executive branch. The president has the power to appoint judges to federal courts, including the US Supreme Court. And one of

The House voted to impeach President Clinton in 1998. The Senate later found Clinton not guilty of the charges against him.

the courts' roles is to decide if actions taken by the president are legal.

Impeachment

Congress can remove a president from office for serious misdeeds. The House of Representatives can vote to impeach, or charge the president of wrongdoing. If the House votes to impeach, the Senate holds a trial. To remove a president, two-thirds of senators must vote to convict the president of wrongdoing.

Only two presidents have been impeached: Andrew Johnson in 1868 and Bill Clinton in 1998. Neither man was found guilty. Both finished their terms in office.

In 1974, Richard Nixon resigned rather than face impeachment in response to his involvement in illegal activities that took place in 1972.

The president is at the center of the executive branch. This branch plays

Nixon's Resignation

On June 17, 1972, several men were arrested for a break-in at the Watergate office complex in Washington, DC. They were caught stealing secret documents at the Democratic Party's headquarters. The men were no ordinary burglars. All had ties to President Richard Nixon's reelection campaign. The reasons for the break-in are still unknown. Later it came to light that Nixon had taken steps to cover up the break-in. The cover-up was a more serious crime than the break-in. It became known as the Watergate Scandal. In August 1974, Nixon resigned rather than face impeachment.

The president both lives and works at the White House. Every president has lived at the White House since John Adams in 1800.

an important role in governing the United States. But it must work with the other two branches to keep the balance of power in check.

President Franklin Roosevelt's speech to Congress after the attack on Pearl Harbor is famous. In this part of the speech, Roosevelt described his actions in response to the bombing:

> *As Commander-in-Chief of the Army and Navy I have directed that all measures be taken for our defense, that always will our whole nation remember the character of the onslaught against us.*
>
> *No matter how long it may take us to overcome this premeditated invasion, the American people, in their righteous might, will win through to absolute victory.*
>
> *I believe that I interpret the will of the Congress and of the people when I assert that we will not only defend ourselves to the uttermost but will make it very certain that this form of treachery shall never again endanger us.*
>
> *Source: Franklin D. Roosevelt. "Transcript of Joint Address to Congress Leading to a Declaration of War Against Japan (1941)." Our Documents. Our Documents, n.d. Web. Accessed September 17, 2014.*

What's the Big Idea?

Take a close look at this speech. What is Roosevelt's main point about the attack on Pearl Harbor? Pick out two details he uses to make this point. What can you tell about Congress based on this speech?

IMPORTANT DATES

1787

1789–1797

1803

The Founding Fathers write the US Constitution.

George Washington serves as the first US president.

Thomas Jefferson completes the Louisiana Purchase.

1941

1951

1974

The Japanese bomb Pearl Harbor, and the United States enters World War II.

The government ratifies the Twenty-second Amendment.

Richard Nixon resigns as part of the Watergate Scandal.

1861–1865

Abraham Lincoln expands the power of the presidency during the Civil War.

1868

Andrew Johnson is impeached and acquitted.

1933

Franklin Roosevelt becomes president during the Great Depression.

1998

Bill Clinton is impeached and acquitted.

2000

In a controversial election, Al Gore wins the popular vote but George W. Bush wins the presidency.

2009

Barack Obama is inaugurated as president.

Take a Stand

This book discusses the Louisiana Purchase. Do you think Thomas Jefferson should have made this purchase? Or should he have waited for the Constitution to be changed? Write a short essay explaining your opinion. Make sure to give reasons for your opinion and facts and details that support those reasons.

You Are There

This book discusses how Congress and the executive branch work together to pass laws. Imagine you have been elected president. Congress is debating a bill you do not like. Do you try to convince Congress not to pass it? Do you use your power to veto it? How do you think the public will react to your decision?

Say What?

Studying the executive branch can mean learning a lot of new vocabulary. Find five words in this book that you've never heard before. Use a dictionary to find out what they mean. Then write the meanings in your own words, and use each word in a new sentence.

Surprise Me

Chapter Four discusses the job of the president. The way the president is portrayed in the media can be interesting and surprising. After reading this book, what two or three facts about the presidency did you find most surprising? Write a few sentences about each fact. Why did you find them surprising?

GLOSSARY

bill
the draft of a law presented to Congress for consideration

convict
to find or prove guilty

department
a division of the executive branch of the federal government

dictator
a person who rules with total authority and often in a cruel or brutal manner

foreign policy
the plan or method for how one nation deals with another nation

impeach
to charge a president formally with misconduct in office

negotiate
to come to an agreement on an issue after having a discussion with a person or a group of people

segregation
the separation or isolation of a race, class, or group

succession
the order of succeeding, or coming after another person or event

treaty
an agreement between two or more countries

veto
the power to prevent legislation from occurring

LEARN MORE

Books

Cheney, Lynne. *We the People: The Story of Our Constitution*. New York: Simon & Schuster, 2012.

Lee, George R. *U.S. Presidents: Past & Present*. Greensboro, NC: Mark Twain Media, 2010.

Websites

To learn more about How the US Government Works, visit **booklinks.abdopublishing.com**. These links are routinely monitored and updated to provide the most current information available.

Visit **www.mycorelibrary.com** for free additional tools for teachers and students.

INDEX

ABOUT THE AUTHOR

Rebecca E. Hirsch, PhD, is an award-winning author of more than 30 nonfiction books. She has written for young readers about science, nature, geography, and civics. She lives with her family in State College, Pennsylvania.